A Grammar to Waking

Books by Nancy Eimers

Destroying Angel, 1991
No Moon, 1997
A Grammar to Waking, 2006

A Grammar to Waking

poems by

Nancy Eimers

Carnegie Mellon University Press
Pittsburgh · 2006

Acknowledgments

Grateful acknowledgment is made to the editors of the following journals in which these poems first appeared, sometimes in different versions:

American Literary Review: "Crepuscule," "Photograph of a Young Girl, 1941"
Crab Orchard Review: "Handwriting in America," "Occasionals"
Denver Quarterly: "Nouns," "S-Curve, 131"
Field: "Lunar Eclipse," "Earthquake Memories" (under the title "What Gets Done")
Florida Review: "Clothes on a Line," "So We'll Go No More"
Gulf Coast: "Bygones," "Scriptura Vulgaris," "Thoughts of the Moon"
Harvard Review: "Mall at the Crossroads" (under the title "Crossroads Mall")
Indiana Review: "Arlington Street," "On a Dog Dying in Separate Frames"
Marlboro Review: "The Motion Detector"
Shade: "I Finde in a Boke Compiled to This Matere an Olde Histoire," "If Fame Were Not an Accident, and History a Distillation of Rumour"
TriQuarterly: "The Mercator Projection," "Shower"

"A Verb in This Mood," "At Two," "Detail: Stone Floor, Garden of the Master of Nets," "Driving in Snow," "Hearing Aid," "Passing Things," "Private," "Psychic Photographer," and "Train Whistle" were included in *A Verb in This Mood*, a chapbook appearing in *Black Warrior Review*.

"Passing Things" was reprinted in *Poets of the New Century*, edited by Roger Weingarten and Richard Higgerson.

"Arlington Street," "Mall at the Crossroads" (under the title "Crossroads Mall"), and "Lunar Eclipse" were reprinted in *The New Bread Loaf Anthology of Contemporary American Poetry*, edited by Michael Collier and Stanley Plumly.

"Arlington Street" was also reprinted in *New Poems from the Third Coast: Contemporary Michigan Poetry*, edited by Michael Delp, Conrad Hilberry and Josie Kearns.

I would like to express my thanks to the National Endowment for the Arts, the Whiting Foundation, and Western Michigan University for fellowships that provided me with the time to complete these poems.

For the wisdom, affection, and support of Sharon Bryan, Jim Ferreira, Rich Lyons, Alane Rollings, Mary Ruefle, Betsy Sholl, Daneen Wardrop, Ed Eimers and Jeanne McCormick Eimers, I am endlessly grateful.
My deepest debt of thanks and all my love to Bill Olsen, always.

Book design by Christopher Boette
Cover design by Rebecca Bortman
Cover: Joseph Cornell, *Untitled (How to Make a Rainbow)*, 1972
Kalamazoo Institute of Arts Collection. Purchase in honor of the docents at the Kalamazoo Institute of Arts and in recognition of the 25th anniversary of the KIA Docent Program.
Photo: James Riegel.

The publication of this book is supported by a grant from the Pennsylvania Council on the Arts.

Library of Congress Control Number: 2005924486
ISBN-13: 978-0-88748-447-6
ISBN-10: 0-88748-447-6

10 9 8 7 6 5 4 3 2 1

PENNSYLVANIA
COUNCIL
ON THE

ARTS

I

II

III

IV

Notes

for my sister and my brother

I

A Grammar to Waking

There are so many rules we don't even know.
Page after page

torn out and thrown away.
But we wake to them anyway.

At four-thirty in the morning birches are joined
with the blackness of pines

feathery at the top and solid below
not quite like an ocean,

less voracious
more formal. But the moon

is still attracted, hovers over it.
At seven the trees have separated themselves and are fragments again.

Fragments of what?
It is so, so early.

Before I open the window
the pines are rushing just by standing still.

Or nouns make everything rush that is not themselves.
A fragment, I might keep going forever

except for my skin.
In the afternoon

there are waves of tree frogs singing everywhere,
adhesive disks at the tip of the toes,

tiny verbs climbing all over the branches.
The pines are drawers of blackness even in daylight.

They store up intonations that can't be expressed.
Though on our lips is *Fire!*

or *Summer is here.*

The Study of Limits

Into the lateness far out at sea
there may be a drizzle of light
poured down from the moon,
or just black like the sound of which they say
"you could hear a pin drop,"
sound of other tiny sounds,
the papery tick of a watch on a piece of paper,
ratchety spring of the body
turning over in bed.
A pain maybe nagging to be recognized
as specific shape to the right of the navel
is soundless as far as human
ears are concerned. Maybe the illegible screed
of mosquito pumps into the air.
So you are prey and preying
upon the silence that isn't, emphatically
isn't a listener. Thirty-two years
of somebody else's life may be its own
sleep tolling at your side, breathe subside and breathe
like a whisper's bell, but however you settle
it that you love that shape,
that him, you are
outside. What's inside your own,
precise ancestral twinge,
speaks like a small stone
used in reckoning, a calculus,
quaint little milestone on a road
on which you'll never meet.
You could wake him, you could tell that pain
like a bead alone on a string
saying the same thing
to the every night in a single night,
stingy bracelet, plundered rosary bead
with its single deposit of nacre,
small *um* of fear. Your neighbor
in this borderlands is a fact
in the dark, his back turned off
to its math of pain, unplugged
from its own sharp daily nightly voices
and drifting afar but not far enough
away to calculate, clock softer
than any face with its lights off.

Driving in Snow

Deer from dawn to dusk
are snow. All night it snows—
                          or out of the pines
they jolt into our headlights
and are deer again—

hard-bright. Snow never was.
                          Snow closed its eyes in time.

      Do we turn back to spirit at night
      only to find we have a body after all?

I was driving inside a snow globe,
                          treeless, cottageless,
and snow fell endlessly

into the road: that elongation of a dark
too old to be a road, too slow for the driver in back of me.

Maybe you know him, maybe he's flashed
                          that same floodlit impatience
in your rearview mirror.
Did it blind you, did you want to think
the incandescent filaments

weren't twisted inside your own eyes?

I blinked, and he was out of any story
that began *I didn't see the accident,*
just a car,
      two cars stopped beyond the curve.
It wasn't even a story, just a bullet whizzing by—

I saw two figures crouching over something
human, yes, I think.
                          So soft, no outlines—
just a heap of dark. Spirit or body?
                          Did it even know?

Was it, was she, awake inside, or over us?

I seemed to know it was a woman lying there,
some part of her running back into the trees.

Maybe it would have been better to be snow by then.

Maybe she was fine
and sat back up into herself.

Or maybe she was in the air by then,
undestined, anapestic,
                    from a comic opera—

Miss Patty regrets . . .
—soft laugh, when it is time, past time.

The deer are safe now, dark inside.
What I heard is way back in the snowed-on trees

—*hi, sweetie*—
                    it's a human voice—

then it's headlights, looming snowflakes,
tree trunks
                    rushing past on either side
to get out from under it all.

And it is very late now, even in a night of endless snow.

Arlington Street

Some lost trumpet blast from Revelations tucked inside the brain
of an aphasiac.
He laughs
as if his tongue were a siren,
as if his teeth were jackhammers.
I've felt the dump truck of his larynx
churn inside me.
I only know the laugh the way I know the boards in the fence
the laugh comes leaping over every morning, every afternoon,
behind its fence a face
no one has ever seen.
He rambles on that crooked bicycle
of a laugh teetering around a corner, falling off the edge of the joke.
That laugh
of metal stair steps ending midair, halfway up a burning building,
no way down.
Some days he merely growls
the lower notes of an emery board,
as if the trees and houses on this street
were empty. Mereness. Gold and silver numbers
nailed to shingles,
broken porch swings,
hollow trees.
Some days he makes no sound. As if his mouth were gone.
As if he were the bygone hoot of a derailed commuter train.
As if his mouth were trying to haul the rest of him away.

Passing Things

When I hear the sound of someone talking I go to the window.
That's how quiet my house is,

everything holding still
like a rabbit hidden so deep inside itself you could miss it

trembling at the edge of the lawn,
while outside the rabbit, sound goes pretty quietly about its business,

a house finch singing its tangled string of song up in one of the
many thought-cloud trees.

And when a helicopter rips along like a roofer shucking tiles
or a jet unravels a sadness knit of steel wool

these are passing things. These are things taken out of a box
of planets and stars and put back again.

The cat across the street like a pale orange ghost or a puff of smoke
drifts in and out of bushes and stalks the border

between what is private and what is a secret.
The mole and the thirteen-line ground squirrel tried all night to be secrets

even from themselves. But sometimes you have to live in the public eye,
which could be lonely or simply frightening.

A man, a tall man, looks back, talking over his shoulder
to a woman pushing a baby in a stroller.

But "something is wrong with the picture" in *this* coloring book—
no door in a tree trunk or a bird upside down in the sky—

no. I mean their pace is erratic, their gestures too wide. Free and open to the
    public.
The two of them walking single file. The way he's calling back to her.

And how she jolts the stroller over a rut and shrieks,
lifting the baby oh so carefully by its foot.

Then the man stares at *me*—me at my window, bringing up the rear.
I see then he isn't the father. The child is a doll.

Its blank eyes and smile and hard cheekbones preset to happiness.
Its hair spun yellow

like a hank of what fills the room of a fairy tale by morning light,
once straw, now simmering gold.

She lowers it back down into the stroller. As if into bathwater.
And the loud, patient voice of the man keeps herding her on.

But no, she stopped. And stays stopped as a mother bending over a stroller.
For all the world to see she leans into the task

required of a woman attended down a public street:
to tuck the secret in. To make it seaworthy. To smother it.

Photograph of a Young Girl, 1941

1. You know the one. She looks up smiling from the book she is reading. She could not have been reading the sentence I just read by Virginia Woolf: *Every day includes much more non-being than being.* Woolf wrote this sentence in April 1939, two years before the looking up from the book, the smile. But the sentence hadn't been published by then. Woolf died in 1941, and the sentence stayed inside her handwriting, in its past. "A Sketch of the Past." You know the one.

2. She is wearing a watch. She is flirting, really, with the camera, or the eyes on the other side of it.

3. If this were biomedicine, we would be studying a photograph of her eye, so magnified it would give an anatomy lesson: lacrimal punctum, lacrimal caruncle, semilunar fold, gray line, lacrimal lake.

4. We see into the black and white of her, which is something else. A Ferris wheel through fog. The shadow of snow geese passing over but not in the picture.

5. She knows who is taking the picture, we don't, it's simple, she smiles, it must be someone she likes or wants to like her, it must be a relief not to be studying, the watch on her arm doesn't weigh it down, time is simply the time it is on her wrist, nothing worse, a moment of being, and maybe, considering how alive she looks, the next minute will be one too, and the next.

6. The blank pages of the book are so bright they almost pour up from themselves.

7. A book I am imagining to be about light, about the degree of value between black and white. If she woke from her life, she could turn the pages for us, a book of photographs. The close-up of a bullet. The mournful eye of an elephant almost lost in its puckers of hide. The lunar surface of a horseradish. Mottlings on a grain of rice.

8. *I feel that strong emotion must leave its trace; and it is only a question of discovering how we can get ourselves again attached to it, so that we shall be able to live our lives through from the start.* She, Virginia, wrote.

9. Would she want to (Anne)? Live her life through from the start? *Our baker's boy got hold of some sewing silk, 0.9 florins for a thin little skein, the milkman manages to get clandestine ration cards, the undertaker delivers the cheese.* She, Anne, wrote. By now she was in hiding. Writing was being.

Non-being—the long nights? The ultra-quiet days? The being—sounds in the warehouse by night, everyone using the wastebasket for a toilet—the non-being, not being able to flush the actual toilet with workers downstairs by day?

10. Looking up, does she even remember reading? Isn't that joy on her face, maybe the joy of just lifting the head?—movement that abandoned its photograph. If this were not her face but a cross-section of her hair and skin on a slide, the longitudinal filament would be telling us it is not the hair of a mouse or sable or an Indian bat as we look down through the eyepiece of the microscope.

11. Her hair is black. Each shaft as she sits there in living time tugs up blackness out of the light—

12. A word is not remembered, it is not even lost. On the cover of her own diary she is looking up, *my* book on *my* desk, straight up into nothing, the ceiling, smiling, from the book *she* was reading. Or change the emphasis: smiling *from* the book she was reading, because of?—having taken it in. Into the light and fog of her. Look. There are rows of poplars in a flooded field rising out of themselves.

So We'll Go No More

Not the brown creeper, not the pygmy nuthatch, no,
upside down
and skirting any name for anything
up the trunk of a tree.

Not Kirtland's warbler or the tiny community
college in the woods of Michigan

named for that bird which nests in jack pines
sprouting in the wake of fire,

not the rusty blackbird—mobile, nameless
punctuation
on this page of snow—not the evening
grosbeak, its tribe spread eastward
past the Great Lakes to New England now.

Not the old world
sparrows, darting and larking
into trees and shrubs beside our houses
as if leaves had a mind

to come and go. As if the branches in winter
had asked them to.

No. Not the snow finches, listed but
so remote from where we live
they are unpictured, undescribed
in *The Lives*

of North American Birds.
Not the skulking
Bluethroat, not the Asian thrush
or Rubythroat that

at the edge of a thicket
pauses to look back.
Not Say's
Phoebe, soft-voiced, issuing
out of Say long silent
since he uttered this little prophecy
of his "a bird."

Not the quotation marks that ought to go
around the names
birds don't even bother
to fly around in,
away from or with.

No, this *roving*
was a flock of cedar waxwings—
a *they*, an *is*

so late into the night
of afternoon,
the snow so bright in the lightbulb
starkness of a winter sun,

no, not the cardinal's dank red and
not the blue jay's news-flash blue,

this was little candles dipping down out of one tree
and dripping
up into another and down again
into a lowdown tree with berries
dark winter-red,

smallish birds, their flight between two trees
so spare,
into their own

soft colors, grayish-plum
and underneath, yellow
a little less yellow than yellow is.

They didn't do their famous
lining up on the branch to pass berries
cheerily—so we yearn—beak to beak.
Little tallow birds

with wicks on their heads,
not so much alight
as iridescent,
it's quieter.
But *roving*, yes, they were,

indeterminate and yet possessed, a force, if force
is quiet, if quiet is loving,

is it?, it is
out of reach
except by looking up

in the old way, in the old world,
as at the bland
secondhand
light of the moon,

back before
anybody ever walked there—

Nouns

The beauty of the moon is intellectual.
That is, we can't decide exactly what it is
or what, in 1999, to do with it,
the way we can't decide about a noun:
does it name a person, place, or thing,
or is it all a matter of placement, only being what it is
because it's standing next to certain other words?
"Magnificent desolation," Aldrin said.
Sometimes in the TV blitz of memory I'll see
a choir of marines on bleachers singing lustily,
but never "Magnificent desolation."
They sing the sentence Armstrong planned to say,
not the sentence as it was
when it arrived on earth, moth-eaten, shivery,
minus an "a," lost or forgotten in the star-confetti
that alters what is said
between the moon and earth.
Marines in dress whites couldn't sing
the atmospheric disturbances in a human voice
even if they wanted to—they don't—
but they can and do restore the "a" alongside "man,"
having rescued it, bobbing upside down in the waves
of electromagnetic sound, little signal without a job,
giving it back to a man unfixed, unspecified.
Not "*the* man," "*a* man," humbled, hopping around
up there. An "a" is likely to go floating off
but is more close-mouthed than an adjective.
The moon. All week I've been reading about it
and reading is one thing. The moon of 1969
in a newspaper open in your hands this morning
here, inside a house, is one thing.
Thirty years ago the real moon was—
what? Magnificent desolation? In 1999 it's not a place
we want to go. The moon hung over
Hoy McConnell's house, and Hoy came strolling out
as if to ask if I would care to know
its cubic feet and attic space. Did I really do that,
just stand there gazing up into his trees?
That day's a word in progress,
letters missing. Or a miner's candlestub.
Or on a rainy or a snowy night
a stone circle invisible from the road—

you have to know it's there
just off the A10 past Penzance, in Cornwall,
to see it there, in among the twisty gorse.
A place on earth I know the very least about
only from having stood there, spooked, for maybe
half an hour. 1994. Great stones on end. The circle
just kept *occurring* to itself. And time was not
a clock face or a metronome, though time was.
Time was not a mortar or a pounding stone,
though time was. Time was not a verb or a motion;
time was, maybe, what was held
in place—not fluttering, just real.
Magnificent desolation, how long can you go
without verbs? Without an After?—
throwing things out the hatch, boots and backpacks,
empty food and urine bags. There must be takeoff,
being weightless again, and the coming back
down to earth from a thumbnail moon
into body weight and flashcubes and quarantine.
Before they even landed on the moon
—thirty seconds to pass over the rocky place,
the planned-on, deathly landing site,
and find a flatter, safer place to land—
before any Before there is
this present, on its way nowhere as rain or light
or rarely snow occurs to standing stones on a moor: the
this is it. Whether we consciously think it or not.

S-Curve, 131
—Grand Rapids, spring 2000

Because it's dangerous or old, because
it doesn't slow us down, because it ought to be
less drastic, maybe half an O, because we want
to skirt something and live, because no other
single letter tells us there is more,
they've closed the S-curve down. Construction
for at least a year. "A nightmare," says a woman.
"There are people out there working on it
24/7." Meaning in any language I can speak
all day all night seven days a week,
out there when we sleep or wake at night as stars
are out there far beyond our puny streetlight-halo
grasp of them. 24/7—that phrase belongs
to a kind of highway talk, made out of numbers,
letters sprinkled here and there,
S-curve, U-turn, I94, G.R.,
all other words lopped off, a language without
future or history, a freeway, a *now,* bare, digital.
Numeric grace I can't even aspire to.
And yet the S-curve on 131 through downtown
was not one terse unbroken passing through—
too many ornate gasps and swerves and tailgaters
to translate into simple speed. Oh then
the surge of us believed language could be sleeker, less
circuitous, a set of bits each smaller than addressable
memory. Meanwhile inside our cars many
had words, the angry kind; words might drive us
off the road. And to be fair, there were apologies, a password,
song lyrics, maybe a reassurance, a promise made.
Speed would not remember them. The curves would.
Will they be there in a year? How gentled
will that S become? Gentle as speed is,
relegating language to the tires,
to what it always was, humming and repetition.
God speed. His pulse sped up. The days raced by.

Mall at the Crossroads

If I close my eyes, I can picture how it looks in the dark—

rustic benches, Sunglass Hut, Gazebo of the Nape of the Neck
and Bend of the Knee,
pet shop window of kittens draped softly over and under each other
sleeping as deeply as bedroom slippers . . .

this is the living mall, the one with the carousel,
where in the daytime horses ride but not up and down,
they just ride around and around,
happiness put out to pasture.
The faces of the riders are not the faces of children any more,
this one looks embarrassed, that one looks strained.
But at night in bed the spookiness

comes back and restores them to themselves,
and they sleep.

At Abercrombie & Fitch the mannequin on skiis
has Little Orphan Annie eyes.
At The Limited, there are rows of torsos,
sweater girls without their heads,
the nipples hard.

On the other side of town is the ghost mall:
the Department of Public Safety, a movie house
busy on weekends, dead on oceanic weekday afternoons,
stores and stores of emptiness
and at its epicenter, statues: three,
women in Grecian drapery, each one as rapt as somebody who isn't there,
each head untenanted, resounding like an empty dare.
Sometimes, after a movie, I walk around them, in circles,
stand in the path of their forsaken eyes
to sober up
from all that dark.

But the mall of the living, the ruin
built out of someone's recovered memory
of a castle,
parking lot of forgetting all around it:
I could walk through, up and back, criss and cross, with my eyes closed,
the crossroads of my days and nights marked out for me

like the lines on my palm.
I ride the escalator down
to see my mother riding up, opposite me.
Her face turned away from me, it is
the underside of a leaf.

I hear my sister's voice behind the curtain
of the tabernacle next to mine.
Then in my abode I clothe my soul in haste
with a pair of Guess jeans and a v-neck tunic sweater
but when I look in the mirror it is too late, I am drowning in it
and my sister has departed from me,

shirts and pants and dresses shed like skins
and tossed on the little bench and floating across the dead seas
up a stream to a floodplain littered with straight pins.
Wherever she has taken her body
it must be lighter than it was
in the instant ago of our former life.
Into the aether:
into the upper regions of the mall
where Christmas lights are strung. Maybe she is one of the lights

a child cradled in the arms of Santa
looks up at tearily: the face of her mother
snuffed by Santa's beard.

Sometimes I come here just to be a lost mariner
but I am never lost:
there are the snowflakes frozen to the porthole of a jewelry store,
here is the treasure chest open to a single pearl
laid on a velvet slab,
there is the plashing of faces in the aisles
and the row of lockers stuffed with the coats and hats of the drowned.

My mother has picked up one of the kittens
and walks away with it in the crook of her arm,
my sister is trying out the rowing machine
but she isn't getting anywhere
and so the only way I will ever find them is
if everyone else holds still and shuts their eyes
and we disappear
and it is night, and the moon rows over
the gentle waters of the parking lot.

II

A Verb in This Mood

Days when the wind blows verbs out of reach
along the rise and fall of sentences.
When there's nothing to listen to
but my backyard.

And that way of calling an animal
heard over a fence—
peremptory, and inside that, at odds.
Lost friends. Lost articles.
Several children were reported lost
in his voice. One of them
a boy in a blizzard throwing snowballs
into the falling snow
and following them like a road.

And then like a shrug
the boy gone missing. Forfeited.

Why won't the dog obey?
Is there even a dog out there
in the sweep of not being answered?

After that silence drifting over the fence
is something else
belonging to the boy, not lost.
Somewhere out of sight
of whiteness, softness,
is the jotted down
least part of *no.*
Refusal. Of this falling, not one more iota.

The Mercator Projection

The italic hand commended itself to map-makers
of the 16th century because they found it to possess
. . . fluency, legibility, and elegance.

                R. A. Skelton, foreword to *Mercator:*
                A monograph on the lettering of maps,
                etc. in the 16th century Netherlands

As if Kalamazoo were a point on an old Dutch map,
I feel the letters superimposed in italics
across the houses tonight, oblonged and elegant,
tilted right, long ascenders—the *K* and the *l*—
and one long swooping, a descender—the *z*—flying
over and under us, this place we live
all joins and ligatures for once, like a split-rail fence
or the tree branches. No pen lifts or stops in the hand
of this mapmaker. He has us down. And if
we are whatever we've come to tonight,
let them, the letters, hold us in place
for another sixteen centuries. All over town the trees
are coming down, for power lines, for traffic lanes,
for new apartment buildings and little upstart malls, trees
sawn down to the stumps, so the ganglia
of the roots remain submerged, and you feel the sway
of a charmed amnesia underground, forgetting
one charmed thing at a time, a tree, a line of trees
let go and go and go as a hand opened suddenly
lets go its hold on a tugging rope—lets go its place
and the rope is long gone. Tree, lot, clapboard house.
The roots of trees an invisible signature strung out everywhere
in us, under us. If the pen were held
at an angle of forty-five degrees and the letters,
italic, sloped fifteen degrees to the right of the vertical,
toward what margin were we leaning on that
yellowed map? Kalamazoo, are we inching
east to the ocean, straining out of ourselves?
The italic hand should be long, not round, clear letters
without loops. Easily read. Graceful, economical.
Allowing the map-reader to visualize the terrain:
lakes. Trees. Marshland. Long, undetectable rises
of hills. In 1569 Gerardus Mercator
unwrapped the skin of the world from a cylinder.
And he laid it flat. At last you could put
your two palms down on the open page of the world.

You could hold it like the breast of a sparrow
caught between one heartbeat and the next.
Rapt beneath your hands, not even quivering.
And what would you have? Our town tonight,
no other night in history, inside
whose veins the blood of the sentence rules—
inside we are talking to ourselves in run-on sentences
though to the world of sound we are fragments,
names and phrases. "Yes, there is a Kalamazoo."
Last names hitched with hyphens. Crossroads Mall.
Have we ever been otherwise? Two squirrels chasing each other
spiral up and down a tree like a chain of DNA,
pursuing their sentence irresistibly into what
they always are, aloft on trees, corridors
pulsing in and out of themselves, dark and light. Do they
ever stop? I can almost see the one thing streak
into another, but then the tails twitch and they are
continuous, frothy tail to body, squirrel to tree branch,
night to day. All towns on the map of this world,
all the last ragged leaves and the restless bundles
of squirrels' nests—if we talk to ourselves it is
talk like this, chatty, unbroken so we don't lose
the gist of ourselves, so we can be unfolded
and laid down as a single page, can somehow be
the unbroken line of ourselves that will hold on somehow
into the night. You have to prepare your quill
to release ink in a flow but not a spill
said Mercator, who also wrote a treatise on italics
and planned a five-book atlas or *cosmograph*,
but he wasn't spared long enough, mourns Ghim, his biographer,
to trace the movements of the planets and stars
in book four, or, in book five, the world's geography
in a script so precise and continous—no needless flourishes—
that it must be inscribed by diamond point
in some future still to be named
as the sentences spool inside, as we watch ourselves
talk and write our blotted tracks forwards and backwards
to this very moment, here, Kalamazoo, where a
three-year-old child on Wheaton Avenue
crayons her name at the center of a page:
LiLi, a town at the center of pink construction paper,
*L*s backwards, towering, and each *i* powerfully domed,
while all around there are practice *L*s, faced forwards
or tipped on their backs, or maybe they are the afterthoughts,
a flock of seagulls flying off to the right

to a nearby lake or an ocean we will have
to imagine.

At Two

She says *more*
more than any other word.
I can't even think it now
without hearing her
enunciate,
the *o* slid halfway into *r,*
or seeing her
moist lips
perpetually round
as if the rest of her
weren't even there.

More to the emptiness
of the cup or dish,
at the end of a story
or just said up into the air
as she lies on her back
before sleep
because the word
keeps her awake and sleep
walking out a door—

my cue to slip away
home,
cold spring
snow of tiny flowers

falling all over the world
when I turn on the wipers
and drive into
more softly and *who phoned
twice more.*

Scriptura Vulgaris

The bees' calligraphy was partly sound
rising out of itself, a long brown humming
sentence strung out from the bee boxes to the fields
and back again. I could almost hear crossbars and hairlines,
swashes and bowls in that nervous hand.
What was it saying, who or what was it writing to?
We were walking there, he and I taken in
as commas, in and out of the trees and the passing breath
of nutmeg from the spice factory. Today, no living bees—
a few dead scattered around on the hard lid
of snow—and the bee boxes are quiet inside.
Their boards are warped, so weathered-white
I covet them: oh to lug one home and fill it
with anything white. Paper. And maybe the sentences
of bees would have drifted into the weave
like a watermark when I held a sheet to light.
Today I am here with a friend who has talked us
all around the field's four equilateral sides
as the snow goes on, bee boxes sealed by snow,
the field a field of snow, with blackened stalks and grizzled leaves
so wide apart and crabbed I can't read
what they were in summer, green and fringed things
wafted to us, one by one, as wind. The spacing
between things is part of the math of calligraphy,
a covenant between the white and black
to parcel out the saying evenly and then be done.
That stern and simple choice of lettering,
words wreathed in curves or curves squared off,
a human font, a pouring forth, foregone—
yet I have seen the writing under bridges and on walls
of Dairy Mart and the 7-Eleven, on a cardboard sign held up
by a man at the side of Drake and Main
and on a clapboard house that used to be a neighborhood
bar: KiD and freak and I WILL WORK FOR FOOD
and Bar-bee-Q and ROCK OF REVELATION.
Scriptura vulgaris. And what it says is
what my street says sometimes late at night
by streetlight bloom: *olololol*
when all we have are sleep and the speechless
telephone poles. Beside a field of ellipses
and exclamation points my friend
leans her head to a bee box but hears nothing.

Hears through and through the thready boards.
This morning I saw my father's bold hand
disintegrating on an envelope, my name and address
gone shaky, dotting in and out of this world. Out here
I feel a force of utterance, its stalks that opened
their hearts and bled the world black and white.
Utterance tramping along to the bitter <END OF FIELD>.
It's a little ruthless but I want to be as real
as that field of stalks pushing up out of snow
like the wreckage of typeset, some book crash-landed there
all arms and stems, ears and loops and tails.
Or a winter afternoon sent forth as the light
on an envelope tilted in an open mailbox
half-filled with snow. When we quiet down,
do we fade like old typewriter ribbons? Where do we go
when we aren't saying much of anything?
Maybe other voices, other hands in us
take over, going about their business as quietly
as needlepoint. Even as I was all icy cheekbone, forehead,
nape of neck and fingertips and toes desiring heat and light,
 I was laid down as a square of sunlight on a winter day,
I was moving inside all day like warm spring currents under the rug.

To the Voices Over the Fence

As one backyard gives another the pretense
of privacy, and the other gives it back,
one neighbor seeming not to see the other one
as they drift along on either side of a fence,
you voices ought to pay me the compliment
of civil inattention, the gentle lie
of seeming not to hear me over this fence.
But you really *do not* hear me. You do not even imagine me there
because there is nothing neighborly about me,
I don't move or cry or laugh or say a word.
Still, I thought I was something; somehow you should have known.
I am all listening, and you voices all voice;
listening ought to be what voice is dreaming of.
But you make no opening or closing moves.
When you shout, I am as far away as ever.
And then you sink, which ought to be an overture,
a passage to a gauzy, inner place
of whispers, of subtleties and indirection,
a talk that burns so low, so unsteadily
it's almost breath on candle flame, sheer desire—
you half-erase yourself, you shrug,
willing to deny your deepest nature
just to be supremely unaware,
to turn up the boom box on the picnic table,
bitch about endless heat or the endless rain.
Still, something in me answering you anyway
has rocked and sung, has hated the heat, hated rain.
And I have taken liberties,
I have thought of you as part of my solitude,
have known some of you as under the care of you others,
a scared machine-gun laugh under the care
of the boom box, of called-out deep-notes of command
and the soothing washcloth of a woman's croon.
And the shriek I sometimes hear, cry, scream—
too holographic for a name, thing in the air
changing in and out of itself, a high wire act—
as under the care of things more clearly words,
a word without a sentence, too far off to identify,
in length and tone resembling a name.
It held and rocked that scream—shriek, cry?—
it gave itself away to it, *you* did, sense of presence.
If, as I need to believe, we are never

wholly alone, never leave me, especially when you are
not saying anything, when you are all music,
bass notes bearing out inaudibility,
drops of water falling from the eaves,
when you are merely male tones, female tones,
loud, impatient, laughing, careless, tired,
anything that might have been words when it began.

Occasionals
—Moundville, Alabama

Grass blade constellations, tribes of them, tributaries,
continents, now-to-then carpeting, galaxies

the green rolls out, up and over the mounds,
bodies hugged by other bodies, last words inside last mouths.

They lived on top. Or they gathered up there. Openness is left
of whatever built them. As if up is how or why

each of them could reach back around themselves,
reach back of each other, unzipping, to help each other

out of their bodies. Of course we were
occasional too. Walking shadows there.

That green was all the verbiage left now, up and over the mounds,
the chattering grass was no voice at all. Not even voiceless, that

number I couldn't arrive at, little campfires of chlorophyll.
They didn't warm us, we were cold and we withdrew

our hands into our sleeves and clutched the ends.
Clutched against the openness grass-swells seemed to broach

or somehow ride over. At the museum all would be
explained. Why earth was piled over nothing. Who put

the grass back. Pressed it down over any faltering
dirt when time tried jumping over itself. We occasionals

passed like clouds over the face of grass,
toward the museum that would explain everything.

And the light seemed old, clear. You could see far into it.
Tiny fervent bits at picnic tables: kids. You could hear

their brightness like the tiny perfect far-off
v's of birds. Much was said by the hand-cast

modern building, the reinforced concrete. Inside were placards
and implements of stone just a tick apart in time.

But there was a night, behind display glass, kept darkened,
way before towers and palisades, before mounds—

a little village of families winding down for bed,
huts and scattered pottery and a fire,

a little art and a little religion—there was a night—
but the fire, the tiny fire had been rushed out of a cotton ball,

pulled by somebody's hands, not to scale, big hands, recent,
into wisps, a little snow-fire made in our minds,

brief spot of cold, daubed then with paint, neon-orange,
by someone who could see how things might look from far away—

there was a night that asked for this, so little,
fire sunk to a whisper

so no other whispers could blow it out.

Shower

What are we here for? Rain?
Teardrops and spit in a cup?

Snowdrift, a key, a teething ring.
The gifts are handed around in a circle,

patted or smoothed, opened, closed,
held to the cheek, skin-dusted:

receiving blankets, a terrycloth butterfly,
rattle moons and stars, a pop-up book that tells

the dreams of cats. Too many things for the story
of anyone, even a restless baby

American about-to-be. We are like neo-Egyptians imagining
Before, not Afterlife—softness, airiness, pastels.

So to issue into this world the body needs
small things. Containment.

Little hooded flannel gowns
that widen at the bottom, sealed.

Caps. Fitted crib sheets.
And a fuzzy yellow bear to hold.

Though any clutter handed to the infant body
—blanket, note, endearments in Mandarin—

of this other child, this now-3-year-old drifting among us

watching every gift and every glance go round the circle
is unknowable, on this day and continent at least,

this living room inside a house, this town
perched on a river that, talked out,

sometimes goes underground. Our talk
is also small, like sugar orchids nesting on

a plate. This child, if they were actual,

might ask to taste them. But her tongue would find

the petals hard and breakable.
They are lovely. In their archings

reside the six billion uncertainties.

Handwriting in America

My father speaks of a world of things about
to disappear. Libraries. Books.
Letters by mail. "It won't be long . . . ." In the meantime his hand
has a quaver, his penmanship is unravelling
and his numbers break up like the stencilled numbers
on train cars. Spaced wide apart, meant to be read
as the train goes rattling down the tracks.
He doesn't seem to mind the thought of airports
full of businessmen and women all lost
before their palm-sized laptops open like clamshells
in one hand. And maybe he's the true visionary,
seeing words as things not of this world—
as neither things nor nothings but
a kind of upper air, their physical presence
the very least of them and so to be lessened,
stored as close to zero as language can bear.
In this, a tossing out of what
takes up too much space. The bulkiness of paper, cardboard, ink
becomes as the blink of an eye. And if our mailboxes
should rust at the hinges of their jaws,
maybe that will be a matter of no weight,
or maybe this will, handwritings become antique
as Latin *textus prescissus*—barbed wired, so tiresomely mysterious,
unreadable to each other, even to ourselves
when in some future any of us happens on
a stray hand-jotted grocery list and wonders
what did I want that day? In 1894
A. N. Palmer urged on us children and businessmen
conformity to a model, a "plain and rapid style,"
a penmanship for the "rush of business,"
"real, live, usuable, legible, and saleable."
On this October night *Walgreen's* is brooding over us
in cursive, backlit red some graphic artist dreamed
would be to us as someone's true
unstudied autograph. *There is something furtive
about a true autograph* the Victorians said.
*It must have been written in a careless or confidential
moment.* All one lost afternoon my friend and I
practiced copying the autographs of Paul McCartney and John Lennon—
we wanted to travel over and over
up and down the hills and inkblots of their names,
I was the *P* and *l* and *t* and *y*,

she was the *J* and *h* and *L* feeling glorious
as they soared above and below the line.
I'd like to retrace my own handwriting
back to the first time I ever signed my name,
follow the path of the hand on the pencil—
the touch, say writing masters, should be light—
press the pencil down and follow the loops
wherever they'd go, veering wildly,
illegible, unsaleable, back to the first cursive
n I ever wrote across the page,
all the way back to heedless *n*
driving forward, endless, into its selves.

If Fame Were Not an Accident,
and History a Distillation of Rumour

Raw light, erase the north side of the neighbors' house
so I can see inside this morning,
see all motion edged in shame.
See its married prophets arguing in robes of flame.
The waves of heat come billowing. How it must hurt.
But cold wind, blow through the windows into them.
Cold turns the volume down on everything
but thin sounds, it sharpens door slams into sparks,
freeze-dries footsteps over snow to squeaks.
It's not that cold, but with the wind they say
it feels like zero out. They (we) say since yesterday
a man who was married has lost half his name;
before the hyphen there's now a pause
we will all have to try and remember
not to say. Almost hoarded,
almost brought to the lips, brought there and moving them,
just not to words:
we've become, since yesterday, alien to ourselves.
Another man we know *embezzled*—
it's daytime, he's switched off the lights.
The story has him calling up a pornographic image
on his computer screen where he leaves it
all day to be discovered by women
breasting the vasty deep of dusk
with coffee, letters to be signed. The covenant—
that they too feel shame.
Wasn't his taking the money enough for us?
The cold yellow-green of computer light:
we hold it like a firefly inside a jar.
The snow that was melting down the roof
has frozen in its tracks
to ice dams and enormous gnarled icicles
each with a gothic silence stuck inside.
If gossip were the cold wind blowing through town
it might release us all
from the little gusts and flurries.
Gossip, are we on the verge
of your vast exteriority? The porch steps
are shovelled and mute, the cat prints leading over snow
are suddenly gone, as if the cat had been lifted

cleanly out of itself by a hawk so ravenous
it left no trace of blood. Oh man,
it looks cold out even from here,
though when the heat comes on
it comes on like the final exhalation of a Wal-Mart Store.
That's not forgiveness. That's not everlasting light.
Neighbors, close the curtains so your bodies
shine; then we'll close our eyes and seek out the paths of heat.

The Motion Detector

Let the mummy sleep through this light
that shines on her whenever something moves.
My walking into this grotto where she lies.
And let her sleep through any minor dark
that falls when I stand still too long
watching her. My arms folded but not as hers were
formally by someone else into this
last sleep. Of course what she lies in is not sleep.
She is neither dormant, nor folded into herself
like petals at night. Nor is she the quiet aftermath
of a downpour, nor the feeling in the bones
before. The shape of the pelvis told them
she was a woman. That she was a mother,
a certain whitish glow of the pelvic bones
in the x-ray. For any pictures of her
had to be taken through the wrappings,
and so she was lifted tenderly onto a stretcher
to be borne out of town by Mall City Ambulance
to an x-ray lab in Chicago. Having been brought back,
unpacked and laid back down,
in her wooden bed the shape of a body,
the lid nearby, standing upright against the wall,
let her be as an open box dreaming of closure.
Let exposure stand up out of itself,
reach out its hands to find the lid, and bring it down.
And let the cat mummy off to her side
wrapped like a fold-up umbrella
sleep its smaller sleep inside no thought
of rain. Or let it rain so hard outside
moisture seeps in; let rain undo so brief a catnap
secretly, within. The cylinder it is,
a cat with nothing catlike to it, just a something
something, cloth, is wrapped around. And let us not assume
this cat and woman ever met. Two sawdust pillows
under this robotic light's four thousand hourly winks.
Two sequences begun and ended far from here.
While the crossing of shadows the x-ray told us
were her arms
proceeds in time without her to express.

III

Go Slow, There are Children at Play

In other words, Peshawbestown is also where people live,
not just a casino/warehouse of blanking lights and bells
and not just a parking lot where sun pours down on Comfort Coaches freezing cold inside
and riff raff seagulls are drawn to concrete believing it to be water.
This is also tribal headquarters, sunflowers in a yard like a herd of showerheads.
A gas station/foodmart where a big, soft, fat guy there this year and last
but who knows where in the aftermath of this instant hands me change
his glance so swift it might be stealing back the very hope of touch.
Tony Bennett's name on the casino marquee, curlicue to cross the double-t's.
It is even sunlight saddened by sunglasses. And just out of town it is
a cross and plastic flowers laid at a bend in the road. Who cares was it drink, glare, rage,
      fun.
The flowers are permanent—memorial resins, resinoids, proteins and polymers—
because what does an instant have to do with one so beloved?

Earthquake Memories

*. . . they have been referred to as earthquake cottages, wood
shanties, camp cottages, earthquake memories. . . .*
　　　　　　　　—Lester Walker, *Tiny Houses*

1.

The plain sound of voices, no music so bare—
workmen next door
are talking, numbers drifting out of their mouths,
music made of lines and distances
as if the thing they plan to build or repair
is talking through them, clearly, carefully.
It awes me, what gets done,
how, hand and mouth, they'll hitch the undone to the done
the way a whistle pulls its train along.
And then, how soon what's made or fixed,
a chimney, say, goes mute
and rain and snow begin
without any hands
the niggling job of unrepair.

2.

One year the army built five thousand shacks,
fir and redwood, side to side
two dollars a month to rent one fragile
teacup, one earthquake
memory
until around them San Francisco
one brick at a time and block laid over block
could be stacked high and teetering again.
Until then,
fishing shanties, Sunday houses, bandboxes,
bolt-together houses, cluster sheds,
picnic houses, writing huts
and school bus shelters made a city out of crowdedness:
metal chimneys, no side windows,
newspaper and burlap
covering the inside walls, clothes pegs on the walls
instead of closets,
wood or coal stove, chairs and a table, beds,
and, sometimes, rocking chairs.
Always there was the sound of somebody talking or whistling,
snoring, weeping, rocking

in the house next door, the house in back, the house in front—
houses built to creak and lurch along,
listening chairs
in which the body sits apart from light,
or shadow, or
what has been done to it, or what it has done
with metal or wood in its hands.

On a Dog Dying in Separate Frames

Because death happens faster than that.
Faster to turn your head so I do,
swish and I'm out of it
but it's happening anyway and it's already happened.
Only my hearing can't help
going along,
not with the choking but with the voice of a man that's narrating it.
To breathe, to be alive, to live—
his warm breath.
You can't just turn off the television.
Poor stupid dog on the street waking up to its death.
Why can't it pause to rest up for this?
It's happening, I know about it
because behind the narrating voice the dog
is an underneath making no noise at all.
Its flip its fuss is drowned in silences
radiating out from its muzzle.
Who knows what the listener carries away of that in her body?
Doctors can now "see" pain as it's happening
in the brain, so they know it's there.
Inside the dog there must have been gas station lights
clicking on all over the dark continent
of its death. Not like strings of tiny Christmas bulbs,
not like anything that might lead somewhere
merciful. There it is again
in this morning's newspaper and I happen on it,
see it and see it and see it,
a dog dying in three frames,
infinite much of the choking now left out
and no telling how long it took
to crawl out of itself
to a purer airlessness.
Three frames, beginning, middle, end,
three dogs in the throes.
Somebody took the video in the first place
to document one thing, somebody else is using it now
to document that documentation, evidence
of one thing, of another. Chemicals
wrenching a dog out of its life
bodes well for use on humans. Or: chemicals used on a dog
bodes ill for us. "Us"?

The dog can do three simple tricks.
It wakes, it chokes, it curls up upside down.
The other frames, all the other dogs
gone missing, these three just won't get lost.
The middle dog, thrashing,
can't gasp its way into either of the other two
bodies singled out that desert it,
one by breathing in, the other by expiring.

Private

The trees are departures: night after night they have wandered away
from the central point.

That is why someone is cutting them down.

The treetops are seething. No reason for that. They often do.
Wind is air in a natural motion.

Because there are trees, there is this noise eviscerating all stray curlicues
  and silences.

Just now I was trying to read a little,
trying to keep the page to myself

but the roar engulfed the poem, and war engulfed—was it the stand of trees
behind the Pizza Hut? The trees inside that roar were an intimation.

Too shy to come right out with themselves,
they would only suggest.

So I had to put down my book and go outside and look:
I saw two men in a little cup lifted into the trees.

But what I heard was more to the point. It wasn't talk,
it was a mania for clarity:

the roar of teeth set on an endless chain.

The men sawed off branch after branch
but not the way you might have stricken words from a sentence.

It was louder than that. It was deafening.
With their chain saws they worked up into the trees and they worked
  back down again.

We used to sit on the porch and watch the treetops sway and talk,

and time kept changing the subject. A stand of trees is a clock
whose hands fly off as blue jays. Tonight, they will circle the empty spot.

No trees could have told them they would be beside the point.

Now branches are falling one by one, almost slowly

—something private about it, as if it were happening indoors—

not like an apple but like a plume would fall.
Or like the passing of a hat, or a sail—if the world were tipped sideways.

Thoughts of the Moon

Somewhere between the hoverings of the doctor—voice and hands—
and the nasal bone and cartilage
is a perfect numbness: skin without memory.

He and the nurse must pass to it from the outer reaches
of noise, traffic of door and telephone, dumb show of shadow trees—
through the zone of tension

that radiates from the shoulders, jaw and neck.

They must pass down
to the surface of my everything—my skin—
and slice the epidermis horizontally in fine layers.

How many layers deep will we go?
How deep is the skin? And which comes first, clean skin or bone
or stars shining through from the other side?

Two or three hours, maybe, the answer has nothing to do

with the question taken out of the epithelial me.
I hear the scrape of a something on a skin,
not mine just now, it's rented out.

And there are monosyllables. *Dab here. Hand me the—*
what was that? Some instrument with *double-teeth* in its name.

Downward, towards my listening face, he says
Everything we do here has teeth in it.

And parts of me can take a joke: the sad moon smile,
the sleeping nose, the cheeks adrift.
One layer down and he says he's got to the end

and to the beginning of me.
Let's sew you up and be out of here early.

I close my eyes. Where does space begin?

At eighty miles up the sky appears velvet black.
Outside it is a summer day.
I can hear the frail voice of a thread.

Bygones

The eye hath this sort of excitement in winding walks,
and serpentine rivers, and all sorts of objects, whose
forms, as we shall see hereafter, are composed principally
of what, I call, the waving *and the* serpentine *lines.*
          —William Hogarth, *The Analysis of Beauty*

Across the street high-tension wires dip
but not enough for beauty, Hogarth would say.
The line of beauty is a waving line
along the marble torso of a Michelangelo,
up and down our muscles and bones, in the sway
of trees once arching over the corner Pizza Hut
and gone now, released into our minds
where, like threads twisted around a cone,
they can at last be serpentine—the line of grace.
Still, there are other trees; even without them
I could talk about the beauty in what's left;
I'd analyze the poignance of straight lines,
how, from the square of every clapboard house
the mind drifts sideways, as a goldfinch rides
the swoop of its flying song. Inside each line
a secret's warping inward into *C* or *S*
or even the erratic *J.* That secret's alphabet
and not its past grievances is what I'd want
us to whisper to ourselves. The neighbors keep
their own thoughts on beauty, or sometimes they work them
into earth. Then you can see them.
Out of earth they come,
the doric irises, the fiery car crash
daylilies. On Plate i, figure 47,
Hogarth illustrates the serpentine
within a flower hanging open upside down—
each petal, spiraling around itself,
dips partly out of sight and then returns.
Whale-bone of a corset-stay—wavy line—
hip and pelvis bones that, with a little added foliage,
might burgeon into leaf-tip curlicues,
deliver us a living architecture.
Beauty and grace, it is easy
in summer to see you anywhere.
When from my car I saw a walking woman
hesitate before a house with a For Sale sign,

wavy invisible lines hung all around her in the air,
tendrils of doubts and hesitations,
tendrils of the bygone trees, of all that ever happened here
and all that never did, her passing
passing by, her stopping just to stop and think of the possible
rest. But the trees—
I have to say I miss them, don't believe
a word I say—those bygones, not-so-long-gones, trees,
those I-can't-let-it-be's,
that empty sky above the Pizza Hut.
Whatever they took away requires our presence,
and so we imagine them as water shimmering over us
not exactly to get us back to them—
we steal them away, a kind of embellishment.

Vortex

But the water is thorough.

It is not art, it is not life.
It is a disappearance,
which is not a woman.

It is the carrying of her
in our mind: our so many minds.

Mind that made a shrine
with its hands
that live out in the world
of blue and yellow ribbons
and flowers, teddy bears, notes—
out where she becomes woman again.

But the water is not a shrine.

You can toss flowers at it
and they float.
You can stand and look over it.
It is not monument
to her, to her
anything.

A bourne might be,
to meandering. But this is
lake; this is ocean.

Look what it has possessed—
not her and not the holding together
of "her." Just
light where her dark should be;
dark where her light should be.

She is all bones,
she is two skeletons now.
Female. And a "full-term fetus."
They came apart

in the water.

61

It took her some
time but she is immersed in it.
She is, yes, destination or goal.
It's just

that she's forgotten
how to be a woman
going somewhere or being
come unto.

The water is unemotional
vortex. Lemons and golds,
up to the moment news
of the waves thrashing
it out in her.

Nobody says a word about water.
But water made her

shimmery, wavery,
carried her by negation
out of the skeletal "it" hauled out of a wave
as strong wind blows
across a fetch,

as wave
rolls on its orbital path to the shallows
to break on shore
and slide back out.

(Laci Peterson)

hmmm

They All Went

Maple leaves rained on for hours are downcupped, little raincoats over nothing up and down the line. A car pulls up in the neighbors' gravel driveway: it must be noon. If it's raining, it must be eternity in Kalamazoo. April the 20th, 2002, open before me. Tangled-string-song of the housefinch, spring song of the chickadee, shimmery handwriting of the friends and relatives of Augusta, Gusty Wendt, whose book of autographs is open on my desk. This was before she was my father's grandmother, a gust of wind. Heinrich Wendt. Maria Wendt. Minnie Wendt. They all went. That was the joke under my mother's breath when they unrolled the family tree on a window shade and read the names at my father's Family Reunion. *May we rise and dwell forever in the world beyond the stars,* Louise Bectkey wrote. *Ever your friend.* Didn't she, Gusty, want to stop reading after *world,* before *beyond? Menomonee, Wisconsin, 1881.* Spring rain only feels like an eternity. Time for the flock of red-winged blackbirds to pass through the trees all morning, singing over an invisible swamp. Time for a squirrel to run through and through itself across the street like waves and get safely to its other shore. The sundial close-mouthed. There are other ways of telling time: by the lilting train whistle of an ellipsis. Three long tugs, another *now* omitted between Detroit and Chicago. Not just by trains in the act of passing away. By tails and strokes of spray paint on the sides of the boxcars slowed down enough for us to read.

Train Whistle

It's what sound has for a moon.
Early in the morning and late in the afternoon

it rises over us and shines downtown.

And wherever it stops, when it stops,
are we even a whistle stop,

this town of acorn hats and bird droppings?

A whistle might blow us away.
Each morning and afternoon the whistle blows itself away.

At the station a woman I know tightens her hand on a bag.

She is wondering if there will be time to drag
all four suitcases and a cat taxi onto the train.

This waiting—when did it take me? Where will it arrive?

Either way, the tracks curve out of sight.
They say wait. Be in readiness

under a sound made by the lips, a bird,

a wind, a missile.
Something that might not stop here after all.

IV

The Ratio of the Said to the Unsaid

This early fall's a music not yet ready to be
written down,

red passages in leaves still mostly green,
making me think of drumbeats in a requiem

Mozart didn't live to finish,
the ratio of the said to the unsaid.

According to one version of the story, his last act
was to try and say those drumbeats

with his mouth, someone else listening,
who would later write, "*That* I can still hear."

Not remember. Hear. Her, the listener's, subtext being,
whatever else has passed away—

things she, Mozart's sister-in-law and nurse, couldn't be
expected to recall, time in any one

of its little wayward drifts—
those drumbeats *are*. Now *were*. Are not again,

but *seem*, to me,
like something the trees are just beginning to reinvent

out of last year, though red doesn't finish the story
and it isn't emotion. Just an astonishing clarity

leaf by leaf: for a little while
it is fall in the twenty-first century.

Women fast-walking in two's are talking by.
I see them every morning from my window,

or walking ahead of me as I walk, always in twos,
and I am twin to the sight of them,

or, walking, twin to passing houses and to chicory by the roadside
even now, this late into the year's late light,

twin to half-heard words, breath-vapor, walking's labored silences.
A foghorn speaks to another bigger foghorn,

maybe the ferry to Whidby Island:
talk, it seems to me,

is an asterisk, not quite passive,
poised, hovering, omitting nothing on purpose,

a sign of itself, nothing requiring a footnote of two
who will surely circle by again,

ferry and island,
or the women walkers

moving through what must seem like *the actual present*
—have they really accomplished it, gotten there, with their walking?

They fill it in endlessly
with scenery and speed and all that sundry talk.

Maybe they are gossiping, or discussing the orange light
of pumpkins in a nearby field they saw—I saw—

first the color like something spilled out of a vial,
then the *round* containing it

—this is like jumping rope, trying to enter into the twirling
poem that has already begun being spoken—

or they are saying just anything, talking fast to get to
the next thing to say, or faster to what they might never

arrive at: the hugeness of not even talking . . .
empty pages, those spaces pigeons leave between them

on a telephone wire,
spaces that get smaller the colder it is.

Did Mozart have a sense of someone else in the room
when he said what he wanted

the drums to say?
Who knows what dying meant

or how solitary it was or is to be—
words or notes speak nothing of the kind

of silence that must reside in the body by then.
Some mornings an old woman passes, walking slowly by with a limp

as if with each step she left
some part of herself behind.

Any minor loneliness I feel—
on a walk alone, before a television, in a waiting room,

watching other people talk—
doesn't even come close.

Out past the suburbs of high and low tide
bell buoys are rung by the jostling

waves and wind whose invisible signatures
are remarkably alike;

there's a stuff like angel hair hanging over the water
of the Sound,

so bright I have to shield my eyes from here
just to see the radiance,

and all the while
not the foghorn or bell buoys stuck in place

but the ferry filled with people
staring out side by side into blindness

is pulling for shore.

Remorse

Everything you don't like about yourself seems the essence of you.
It comes on like Mozart's *Confutatus*, drums under voices and
        instruments,
punching the lights out of consolation and repose.
Until death seems less and less a human thing,
too vast for any way we could possibly feel about it.
It is bright out; maybe that is what woke you.
Brighter than a definition of night, or dark.
Branches of pine trees, clouds, whatever they are between you and the
        practically audible moon,
lit hazes, billowings: we need a smaller dark in which to sleep.
But there is nothing human out there obstructing the night,
the only house nearby is dark, partaking of it, not even dark itself,
        merely
invisible. The campsite down the road is only the thought of tiny,
        multiple darks,
sleepers in tents each a sealed envelope, a kite flown off
its tether, browsing around in utter thoughtlessness, clouds.
It ought to have nothing to reproach you with, this night.
Spurts of scenery are remembered from the day,
sunlight playing the notes of dollhouse gravestones in the little
        Czech cemetery,
down one hill, up another, trees and apples in them,
little stored essences. This night's remorse goes all the way back to
        high school,
up and down the hallways, bickering with lockers, bells, mazes of
        conversation,
the said, the unsaid, down one hill and up another.
Every one of those lockers is a little clamped-shut mouth,
or it is gaping open, foolishness and malice everywhere,
each mouth a fortress having taken itself, unmercifully,
by storm. *Through my fault, through my fault, through my most grievous fault. . . .*
In mass, elder parishioners would say that, beating their breasts
        softly with a fist,
though to you it was sheer rhythm, which was passionate.
Then, when the other voices sink back down to almost inaudible—
it is amazing how light a sound the choir of male voices can sink to,
how low Mozart can turn that human silencing—
that too is a gliding down a hill, in the car today as you turned up the
        volume,
then turned it down again in the nick of time, so the huge upswell
        didn't drown you out,

or now in bed, as you turn one way and another, the pillow scratching
        your cheek,
though to the hand the pillowcase feels smooth.
Remorse. Even under the wind you can hear it. Pine trees, clouds
are saying it. You need some human noise to prove it wrong, confute
        this message from the moon.
The reverb of an outhouse door, a flashlight clicked off in a tent,
some car or train to silence its long-playing, migratory glow.

I Finde in a Boke Compiled to This Matere an Olde Histoire

. . . reading my husband's starred copy of History

Measured by human reading time, they are old stars. Something that belongs not to the past but to us though I wasn't there yet. Left-handed stars, each begun and ended at its radiating upper point. Often the lines don't meet, the star stays open a crack. Or the line continues through itself just below the place it started and the star opens up again. I don't want to make too much of this, just everything. *Historein, historia. To inquire.* Greek and Roman and Midwestern history. Athens, Florence, Des Moines. *See Weid–. To see.* Sometimes a star nearly flies or shrugs out of itself, sometimes there's a pock at the first/last point, where the pencil first hit the page or where it lifted off, which was it, twenty years ago. "Almost 80 of the poems in *History* are new," Mr. Lowell is quoted as saying on the back of the book. Before we went inside the house on Hol Hi Avenue, we wanted to buy it just because it bordered on a quiet with trees. And because of the name of the street. Once inside we didn't like the house; we adored the view. *View, vista, vision* are some important derivatives. *Survey, idea, history, story.* And *penguin* from the Welsh *gwyn–white.* The page of my Jane Austen was filled with snow, the only sound the clinking of her bracelets. Where I came from you don't write in your books. He is part of his time, she is part of hers, though time gets dark at the top, I can't see into it. It's OK, I can hear him in the kitchen chopping kale exactly now. No, it is the smell of onions drifting to me. *Evident, interview.* Entre, between, plus voir, to see. A history isn't windows and trees. To write truly the history of last week, we would meet, some he and she, light years ago in Des Moines, Witmer Pond, put our bodies on in a light wind, put on all they have to say under one of the trees, open the book—not the trees, don't carve names on them—and start writing all over it.

Psychic Photographer

My art is to develop what I didn't see:

I didn't see the dead, but here they come,
rods and globes where there were none,

fuzzy columns, ectoplasmic doodlings,
p-l-e- or h-e-l- across the flowered wallpaper . . .

O light that darkens, hours later, on the negative,
O light only a camera sees,

I don't know why you bother me,

initials hovering over the teakettle,
mist-woman draped across my mother in the easy chair—

I didn't try to draw you out or trick you
into what can look like lung tissue or egg whites in the final prints

any more than I would try and scare a ghost
out of the trees each time it rains

and trees recede. You sign a name, you sit down in a chair,
you darken *me*, is it to—

happen?—once more
stuck in time,

to be a face and hands occluding light—

*

—while couch, piano, chairs and bric-a-brac
glow white,
my living room
refurnished out of light.
Can you tell me what happens
to make that inward, late-night hush?
The living wait
out there in the actual living room—
my mother playing "Claire de lune"

but from the dark side of the moon,
foot pressing the mute pedal
—where are you, can you hear?—
father and sister reading on the couch,
crime novel, mystery.
My brother and a friend, grinning embarrassedly

at what fools light will sometimes make
of handsome men.
And yet, blotches of light and dark,
do you think it's really *you* they want to see?
Sometimes above their heads, beside them
or over their faces
I'll see your faces bloom like kettle steam.

And so you happen as rain falls

invisibly at dusk
before someone has felt the urge
to move, to turn stillness back into a hand,
to lift the hand
and turn a lamp on in the living room.
I walk out of one darkroom
into another, the one they haven't noticed
they are sitting in;
they look up, startled—when. . . ?

Ghost weather
they could perish in.

*

The trees out there in steady rain
are co-walkers,
you mothers and fathers, sisters and brothers,
ebbing in the dusk.
If I should take your picture now,
walking away, halfway from light to dark,
what would you make of me, if you were the rained-on trees,
me with such a strange contraption for a face—

a body with a shadow on its mind?

Hearing Aid

It looks like something Joseph Cornell might have pocketed
not for a shadow box but to keep:
in a pillbox or
a roll-top cubbyhole. Flesh-colored,
thumbnail-sized. A plastic boat
at the mouth of her ear canal.

"It looks," my mother says, "like a blob of wax."

      —Why do I so want it cupped in my hand?
Her mother left her a tiny address book
with a gold notch
set at D,
and a single pearl on a thread like a baby tooth.
Oh, and a pocket calendar from the Drake Hotel,
with January 1 circled in red. Her wedding date? Her period?
Time made so many little stops:
train time. Curtain time.
"You girls need to think about what you want."
She means her watch and rings, the pig-shaped cutting board,
her mother's mink stole fashionable only
to a Barbie doll.

               The hearing aid
has a tiny door in its side.
What's inside, all the things she is thinking.
I want to pry it open so I can hear my voice
or is it my sister's,
or "Autumn Leaves" playing darkly now on the piano,
or brightly as my mother has always meant to be playing it?
In falling leaves
no time, no dark. No way.

She might as well be telling her daughters
I won't hear of your going.

Sometimes I rifle the box of our inheritance,
stealing through my grandparents' Book of Accounts—
grocery lists, how much they spent each day of the week—

there will be a lunch for the Little Flower Circle,
friends of the parish of St. Theresa, next Tuesday,

eternity. . . .
They must have willed their questions somewhere else.

February 4. Eight goldfinches at the feeder this morning.

Jim's mother, dying, lifted her head
when she heard her name—
is it true that hearing comes back at the end?

April 2. Nuthatch at the feeder.
March 21. Robins sing in the early morning now,
though it's cold again. Those are my own notes
already looking back:
no time, any time.

There's a tiny wheel my mother turns with her fingertip
to adjust the volume. Some days
the world just buzzes—
       battery running down—

March 4—spring song of a chickadee—

and she pulls it out of her ear by some kind of
tiny jewel on a string
and puts it in a tray like an earring
whose twin she lost.

Crepuscule

after Bonnard

I.

That was our way:
standing inside a half-built
house looking up
through the skeletal roof.
Were they looking up to imagine
twilight games of croquet
on a depthless lawn,
striped balls rolling in and out
of sight?
All I know is each week
they would visit the glimpse
the house was, each week shrank it
into a photograph crimped at the edges,
small in the palm of a hand.
Later, after the walls closed up,
says my friend Daneen
of *her* childhood
house, it seemed miraculous
all that space could fit inside.
There was room after room of it.
Even the furniture couldn't displace
the stars, lit dust
of the Milky Way, the weird stillness of
true space. Oh
my father, oh my mother,
I almost can't sneak a look at you
looking up—
if you knew would you blush? should I?
A waving *line of beauty*
rose and fell in you.
If you happened to gaze any lower than clouds
you must have seen another almost-
house and through it
other houses and others and others—
not one ready for your nakednesses.

2.

Hogarth made a study of beauty—of lines, of the line of beauty. Curving lines
which serve to raise the ideas of bodies in the mind. He traces curves in the out-

line of a bell, a frond of splashing water, muscles wrapped around bone, up the neck of a woman in the act, *lines thus constantly flowing, and delicately varying over every part of the body,* of turning her head. How long will it take her? The neck a mesh of lines pulled into curves by its swan-like turn. That turn is slower than the time it takes the Northwest commuter train to travel out from the Loop, from east to west, no, northwest, to Des Plaines, town of our starter house, town named for plane trees—incorrectly—they were sap-bearing maples along the river, trees full of water, town called variously *Eau Plaine, Aux Plaines, O'Plaines, Des Plaines.* Pronounced by us as a single word, DssPLANES, a hiss then a spilling. Trees that flowed past all the clutter yet to come—Nuclear Chicago, DoAll, Littlefuse, USA Movers, Motel 6, SUBWAY, U-Haul, RE/MAX, the Gap. This was years away. My sister and I get off the train, in our forties now; my mother sketches my sister's wedding dress for me, in frothy pencil, on drawing paper so heavy it registers every feathery smudge and erasure, what passed, swan-like, from her vision, what was thought better of. A lovely unscribble of hair, a lonely shoulder floating over the dress. My sister travelling towards her wedding self all the way *to the fingers ends.*

3.
Playtime in our bedroom, the door closed,
space was square and dolls filled up with their own hollowness
what you could see if an arm or head came off
or by staring deep into an eye—

you could see something back there
you couldn't see anything.

Like that black dark when at night the lights first go out
and you hold up a hand you can't see
but you know it feel it there
it is yours it is part of the dark.

Like the thought of how the dark
hills at the end of the bed
are the stuffed cat and bear and the autograph hound

whose signatures—the names of our friends—
are squiggles of dark in the dark.

                              Our brother in the next room his door
closed
must be asleep in the upper bunk.
All night inside his head and inside mine and Kathy's
and the heads of our sleeping parents

so he told me once
go all the words we each spoke during the day,
pass through us and are forgotten and gone

so that on the morrow

thinking back is like reading a note
made of spaces cut out of the page.

4.
Crepuscule. In English we say *twilight, dusk.* My godchild pulls her blanket
over her head and says *I'm gone. Gloaming, nightfall (evening). Twi*—two, half.
See *dwo*—important derivatives are *two, twelve, twilight, biscuit, twist, twice,
twenty, twine, between, twin, binary, combine, twig, diploma, deuce, dozen,
dual, duet, double, duplicate, doubt, dubious. Liht*—light. See *light.* We don't
have time. The Bonnard painting is subtitled *La Partie de croquet.* There are
splotches of darks and greens that are night and trees; and splotches of cream
and olive that are men's suits and women's dresses and a dog; and checkered
splotches, black and beige and night-green, fabric of another woman's dress; and
brown splotches, women's hair come loose—they are dancing off to the side; and
splotches of orange, the sunset through the near-black trees or clouds. And the
two last wickets, lined up in the grass so that we can see through them to grass.
And the three brown lines, one almost at the center, that are croquet sticks. I can
see one striped croquet ball, and a brown splotch that might be another. Maybe
someone else can spot more.

5.
My godchild draws my hair
in coils, one heavy blue line coiling down
each side of my pink face
down my body—all legs—
I am going somewhere—
to my huge pink shoes,

my shapes and colors
flooding into each other, my near and far
get married,
marry everything in this world.

My love and I married.
No, we have no little ones of our own

but that is not the way I answer that.

Our godchild pulls
her animal blanket over her head
and says *I'm gone.*

Oh mothers and fathers, o without the h,
o house street star child space true space.
A hand or face
or river or a star our house and suburb
hung upon is a thing
hung by a string,

thing on a mobile swinging by
a child's grasp,

that little grasp that we will ever be
the mother and father of—

so far there's nothing but sky
on the other side of it.
Twilight. A glimmering
of the wickets.
Oh my parents, your small lot
turns inside out

to trees, chairs, stars, beds, TV trays.
From upstairs in my head
these things were placed on the lawn
by a child's hand. Mine, or the hand

of Kathy or Bill.

Clouds, Rain and Snow the book
we read together every night
is turning its pages back.
The families are little,

shovelling snow,
kids with umbrellas, a woman
in a floppy hat. Big fern leaves of frozen vapor
pressed to the window,
our family a geranium in a fishbowl
turned upside down
so drops of water form on the glass
from the skin of the leaves.

When water stands in an open glass,
little by little it goes
up into the air.

On clear nights there were stars and
all of us outside on the grass.

Detail: Stone Floor, Garden of the Master of Nets

—Suzhou, China

I look out of a thousand grays
that memorize a face:
twenty-five years ago I met someone,
and here you are, my husband,

walking back and forth
on the other side of this world,
looking down at the floor
and it isn't even amazing,

luck, longevity,
patterns arranged in tiny, inlaid stones.

I think we would have to be colorblind
to see them perfectly:
a fishnet,
a circle of bats—good luck—
and a crane in the center—long life.

We have had to piece them together
out of beiges, grays, light browns and dark whites.

To see through colors to texture, to see through light

to sheens and dullnesses of stone,
the surge of stones turned in a single direction,
the splash when they are combed apart,

to undergo
light, shade, and form without their colors,

must be a kind of nightfishing—
to spear the flying fish beneath the waves
while flashlights have to wait for them, to spot them when they fly.

A fisherman, the master of nets, had this garden built—
though *built* sounds wrong
to Westerners, to us,

more used to *grow,* the flux
of gardens and economies.

If anything, this garden has worn smoothly down
since it was made.

Our friend who came, as friends come, out of nowhere,
hoists her baby up to kiss her face that was
a stranger yesterday!—
a lifting of eyebrows,

a looking out
of not having
words for things.

We can try to look back *into* that,
we can't go that far back to ever
being in that infant place. . . .
August in Suzhou: do you remember trying

not to move? Heat and moisture
made a cult of stillness.

It was restful not to move.

And yet I felt a force,
almost an ardor—
someone else's, ours,
the holding still, the holding together—

which came first?—

some order
gone

when I turned my head.
Over the depths
each stone had fallen to
your face skimmed towards me.

Lunar Eclipse

Tonight as the merest ghost of us
passes over the moon and washes its face
a dirty orange, we have to try and spot the instant of eclipse,
though some change moves at the speed of flowers, not of something
counted into the hand, so maybe all we'll see
is all we ever see, what's happened
and is done with us,
bygones be bygones,
hands washed, period, end of the line,
a copper moon, then a dun moon, then a pumpkin moon,
fed up and sickly moons whose parent moon is still a mystery,
we the puzzled look on its face,
dead seas blind to our own faces,
deaf to what stone circles want to ask
an ancient smile drawn with a stick in the dust,
our breaths cartoon clouds wisping Earth,
where yellow streetlights are the dotted lines
that hold streets true to their course all night,
our voices one voice, high and low tones in the dark,
waking Marcus the pony at the fence, feet shuffling
to walk the long way back to sleep,
along the lane, beyond the glow of Carbis Bay, over the stars,
around Knill's monument and up the tors
where it will finally be black
whether our eyes are open or closed.

Clothes on a Line
—Zennor, Cornwall

Sometimes those sheets and pants and shirts would travel miles,
over the moors to Gurnard's Head and out to sea,
if you could have read the meter of the wind.
But clothespinned to the line, they had to travel in place,
wind flipped them over and over the line into bundles
we unwound later down to emptiness
and we wore and slept on all the week.
I remember how heavy they were at first, tangles dragged wet
out of the washer that would roar like the engine of a jumbo jet.
I lifted a sheet in my arms, I held the shape of our bed
but it spilled out on either side, our sleep unwieldy now
without us. Arms and legs of clothes
were like a seaweed turned to lead.
As I lifted this heaviness, tried to pin it taut
as something that might actually lighten and dry,
Pip, our landlady, was rooting around in the garden, weeding, planting,
        I didn't ask,
she was talk and cheer, dressed in an old brown sweater.
Jumper, she called it. Even the names of clothes had motion in them.
If you looked beyond the garden to the moors
you could see the argument going on, lightness and heaviness,
wind and the dug-in spiky gorse, the bracken and stones.
Sometimes the geese took a notion to fly, but their wings were
        clipped.
And the shire horses loped outward to the wire fence
as if they could run it larger, run it out of existence.
At first I didn't think I could stand it,
shrillness at the crack in the door all night,
everyone wearing their jumpers even indoors.
Wind drove us out of there in the end, but a colder, later wind,
and even where we moved to, a warmer house in town,
you could feel the numbers spooling up and up
when you started the argument with hanging clothes and sheets
        on the line.
You fought them up there and they frisked all day
and night, too, if you left them there.
And if it rained, it rained, and the crows had a few harsh words
for that and a way of shivering up there on the telephone line,
clutching the miles in their claws as the talk raced either way.
I talked to my parents back in America every week,
but their voices came as afterthoughts,

those blank, unbidden instants in a transatlantic call,
so I looked out on the turnip field awaiting my turn
and trying to bespeak the words that would change the orangey turnips
        into sunsets
just as at that moment they appeared to me.
Cheers, they say in England. Thanks. You're welcome. Cheer.
We left Boswednack because of the cold,
and because of the teenagers doing Tai Chi right out our window, close
        enough to touch,
and the drumming sessions at night in the barn.
And the cold—but we stayed through cold October.
Out there at night our sleep was deep, and the stone house
creaked like a ship inside, rocked and navigated
rampant grass, and the stones didn't sleep,
and the horses fell down into the depths of their snores,
and Pip and her Mum in their nearby houses
and the two kids renting the shed
sailed in the same direction we did, and the stars hung on.

NOTES

"Driving in Snow" is for Patty Harmon.

"The Mercator Projection"—some of the information was taken from A. S. Osley's *Mercator: a monograph on the lettering of maps, etc. in the 16th century Netherlands.*

"Scriptura vulgaris" is the form of inscription brush-drawn as graffiti and signs on the walls of Pompeii. It is characterized by the roughness and vigor of its lettering. The preserved Pompeiian inscriptions include advertisements, election slogans, and dirty jokes as well as quotations—and misquotations—from Ovid, Lucretius, and others.

"Occasionals" is for Bill Olsen and Mary Ruefle.

"Handwriting in America" takes its title from Tamara Plakins Thornton's book of that name, in which Thornton quotes the comment on the true autograph.

"If Fame Were Not an Accident, and History a Distillation of Rumour"—the title quotes Thomas Carlyle.

"Private" is an homage to John Ashbery's poem "The One Thing That Can Save America."

"The Ratio of the Said to the Unsaid"—the description of Mozart's death by his sister-in-law as found in Maynard Soloman's *Mozart: A Life*. The poem's title comes from a passage by Don Ihde in his book *Listening and Voice: A Phenomenology of Sound.*

"I Finde in a Boke Compiled to This Matere an Olde Histoire"—from John Gower.

"Crespuscule"—italicized passages in section 2 are taken from William Hogarth's *An Analysis of Beauty.*